The Apostolic Mantle

A Strategic Company Arising

From The Message Builders Series

by

Mike and Andrea Brewer

Connect with us at

RNetwork.org or RainNetwork.org

The Apostolic Mantle

From The Message Builders Series

Mike and Andrea Brewer
P.O. Box 5945
Maryville, TN 37802

ISBN (978-0-578-20868-8)

Printed in USA

Table of Contents

About The Authors

Mike & Andrea Brewer

Mike and Andrea are, first and foremost, mom and dad. From there, they are the authors of Pioneering Faith and the senior apostolic leaders of Reach International Ministries. Since founding the ministry in 2009, it has grown exponentially by initiating two church-planting movements exceeding 2,000 churches, founding two children's homes for orphaned and abandoned children, birthing a remote medical facility, and launching several other ministries and missionaries throughout the nations.

After having lived internationally as missionaries for several years, their global vision is to see revival and awakening released in cities and nations. They practically work towards this goal by raising up young men and women to release the Kingdom of God here on the earth.

This is done by demonstrating the goodness of God through healing the sick, deliverance, and releasing the prophetic destiny of others by speaking at churches, conferences, and leading international missions teams. In this teaching, we are going to introduce you to the apostolic mantle.

Testimony - Raising The Dead

In the first part of this teaching on apostolic ministry, we will talk about establishing the atmosphere and culture of heaven. Before we move into those concepts though, I want to share a testimony to illustrate how that can happen. In 2017 at our Reach Apostolic International Network conference in Haiti, we had assembled around 300 leaders together for three days.

We were holding the conference at a hotel in Port-au-Prince. Pastors, leaders, and fivefold ministries from all across Haiti came in and opened up the conference with us. I preached on Lazarus, the resurrection power, and how God was raising up and awakening people out of their sleep with this same resurrection power. For the next five hours, the Word of God went forth. It was word after word after word, followed by worship and then more word. It was a powerful time as people began to receive breakthrough. Healings began to break out in the congregation, and the presence of the Holy Spirit was heavy.

Later that day, we had a blessing of the generations. Malachi 4:6 talks about restoring father-son relationships and how vital this is for releasing generational blessings in order to bring forth the destiny in others:

"He will restore the hearts of the fathers to their children and the hearts of the children to their fathers, so that I will not come and smite the land with a curse."

The seed of generational transformation is found when the generations come together which will result in a release of wisdom. The new generation coming up is the answer to the prayers of the older generation, and a meeting of generations was taking place before us. We finally closed out the first day of conference. As we were getting in the truck to leave, a great commotion suddenly erupted over by the swimming pool.

In third world nations, often when someone dies, there is great wailing and mourning. Right there in the hotel, people had just started wailing and crying, screaming out, "She's dead! She's dead!" A woman had been found floating in the swimming pool. Nobody knows for how long she was out there alone, but she was swimming while we conducted the conference. In the midst of this wailing and screaming, others rushed over, pulled her out of the pool, and started pushing on her stomach. They didn't know CPR or any other means of resuscitation.

The pastor that was with us was an EMT for 14 years. Pushing through the crowd, he checked for signs of life in the woman. His voice broke with emotion as he said, "The lady has no pulse. She's not breathing!" I finally turned to the crowd of people standing around us and demanded at once: "Stop saying she's dead! Start praying!" We all started praying. One minute passed. Two minutes passed. Several minutes slowly dragged by. The pastor was holding her head while I knelt at her side. I remember crying out at the top of my lungs, "Resurrection power!!" Suddenly, she coughed explosively, and blew water out of her mouth. She started breathing!

However, she was still unresponsive- not moving. There was no response except for that labored, tortured breathing. We put her in the truck and took her over to a clinic near the conference and went back to our mission house. All the intercessors gathered up, and we started interceding and pressing in for this woman. An hour and a half later, with the afternoon sun hanging low in the sky, the pastor went with Abraham (our spiritual son) over to the clinic to check on the woman. The rest of us stayed on the floor at the house just crying out, warring over her life. Those pastors and other leaders had come to the conference, and we had preached resurrection power as God's Spirit had moved

6

mightily. What would their testimony be when they left conference and went back to their churches? We refused to let the testimony be, "Well, we walked out after the first day, and a woman was dead after we had preached resurrection power and the powerful moving of the Spirit of God." It was as if a mocking-type spirit just tried to come in and take over the testimony for the entire conference.

The pastor and Abraham finally returned from the hospital with a report. We sat there with this violent, internal struggle raging in our hearts. We believed that had God touched her, but what was the final testimony going to be? Pastor had got more of the story from the woman herself: while we were in conference, an unknown gentleman had brought her to the hotel. They swam for a while together before he retired to his room around lunchtime, leaving her there alone. She couldn't swim. Somehow, she got down near the deep end, apparently lost her footing, and went under fast. It was some time later that people had found her floating.

When we visited the clinic the next day, the surgeon came out to speak with us. He told us then that she had certainly died because although a person's body initially sinks when drowning, it comes back to the top after death. The report? She was awake now and starting to respond, so we went and visited her. We sat at her bedside, reveling in what God had just done. She didn't know who we are. She didn't even remember being at the pool, but she laid there in the hospital bed talking to us. She told us her name; her mom came in with her sister and her cousins. The whole family crammed in the little, hospital room! This was the testimony of the town, so we blessed her, loved on her, and then left.

The next day, she and her family came to the conference. She entered the room and made her way up to the stage. Fingers pointed at her from across the room- pointing at the miracle woman now walking before everyone. An expectant hush fell as she finally approached the platform. Turning to look out at the sea of faces, all she said was, "Mèsi. Thank you."

She didn't have anything else to say, so we broke for lunch. I just sat there, physically and emotionally spent. I had been crying and praying for two days. As I sat there resting quietly and lost in deep thought, a young lady named Evoice walked up and asked, "Pastor Mike, do you want some food?" Evoice was at conference last year. Last year, however, she couldn't speak. She couldn't walk. She was paralyzed, but God had fully healed her. Twelve months later, she was asking me if I wanted some food. As I began to choke up once again, I looked around the room and spotted Luigi (that's the woman's name that had drowned), sitting at a table and eating with her family. See, the devil wanted her dead but she was there, enjoying a meal with her loved ones. Faced with the goodness of God, my tears came pouring out once more. Food was the farthest thing from my mind right then.

I don't know if this woman had brain-wave activity or not, but I know she couldn't breathe. I know that if we had done nothing, she would have remained dead, but prayer brought her back. The goodness of God brought her back. She's alive and well, and a formerly-paralyzed, mute woman named Evoice is serving food to myself and all of these other pastors! That's the power found in the name of Jesus! That's the culture and atmosphere of heaven! That's the divine blueprint!

This was a battle of testimonies. On Monday morning, there was a testimony being spoken over this young lady declaring her dead, and it was testimony of unbelief. It was almost a spoken word-curse, and messages like that have been spoken over so much of the Body of Christ. There's been a declaration- even coming out of some pulpits- of how apostasy is coming into the church and of how lifelessness is trying to fill the church. But there's another testimony that is being released from heaven, and it is the sound of the roar of the Lion of the tribe of Judah!

It's beginning to awaken the saints of God. A great shaking is taking place in their spirit and bringing forth a separation of the testimony that has been spoken over the saints of God. The testimony that has been spoken over some of you, the words of "You're not qualified," the words of failure, and the words of "You don't have the resources," have been ringing in your ears, but God has another testimony. His testimony is based on the blueprint of heaven! The blueprint of heaven says that He has the resources. They have already been set aside. He has the plan, and it's already in place.

He is releasing a structure in which the Body of Christ can host this great army that is rising up: an army that is carrying forth the revival and the sounds of awakening. I hear that as clearly as I hear the music going forth in this place, and the music and the sounds vibrating in here. This is causing a great releasing of the sounds of heaven- the sounds of heaven are calling forth this great army. And I ask, "Will you be a part of that army? Will you stand up and take your rightful place as the sons and the daughters of the most-high, God? Will you refuse to compromise? Will you reject those spoken word curses that just declare gloom and doom?"

I reject that in the name of Jesus! I speak out over my region right now, and I say, "Wake up, oh sleeping giant! Come out of your sleep and arise to the fullness of the call of God! Embrace your destiny!" God is releasing a convergence upon our region, and it's the fires and the flames of revival that is going to wake up some of the church. Some of them are dead, some of them with dried-up traditions, but they're willing to take hold of the mantle and call of heaven. Many are saying, "Take it, and run with it!"

A passing of the batons is happening which is also a merging of the generations. The older ones are saying, "I'm beginning to see the hand of God in this next generation." Even though they look different, even though they talk different, and even though they do not embrace some of our traditions, God is opening up that generation's eyes. They are proclaiming to the younger generation, "You are carrying the promise of our prayers within you!" And now, they are beginning to see those prayers come to life and are beginning to water those prayers because the next generation is the harvest that is being released from our elders.

God is shaking this area. He is shaking a region, but it's not in a judgmental fashion. This is a waking up to destiny because so many of us have just received what we have been told. We have received the testimony of failure. We have received the testimony of "You can't do it!" Those words have rung in our spirit until we have believed them, but that's what a stronghold is. The thing about a stronghold- especially a demonic stronghold (a collection of thoughts contrary to God and His nature)- is that it attracts the anointing. The anointing is what breaks the yoke; it brings forth the manifestation and the release of the anointing.

If you have that in you and you still have those thought processes that say, "How can I carry awakening? Why am I called to this? I don't know if I'm called to this. I just don't have confidence," then listen carefully: I hear the Spirit of the Lord saying that you are the one that He is attracted to! He is attracted to you because you are the one that can release His glory because the world disqualifies you. He is the one that qualifies you, so listen to the Spirit of God. Hear His voice today and say, "It's me! That's me! I am a part of the army that's rising up! I am not going to settle for this tradition any longer! I'm not going to settle for the status quo! I have got to press into the things of God! I have got to press into His presence!"

We must become so hungry for His presence that food is no longer appealing to us. When we get so hungry for His presence, the worship time is no longer appealing to us. We have just got to have Him because it has created a divine hunger inside of us, and the only thing that is going to satisfy that hunger is His presence. It's His presence! It's His presence! It is not singing about Him. It is not singing with people who know about Him. It is about Him! It is about taking Him by the hand and letting Him lead you into all truth and all righteousness.

The world is waiting for the manifestations of the sons and daughters of God to rise up because you carry within you the answer to many other people's prayers from the generation before you. You are the manifestation of awakening, but the generation that is waiting on you, they are empty. They are dry. They are essentially dead, they are just looking for something authentic. They are looking for something that is raw and real. They are just looking for God and are tired of being told about Him. They want to experience Him. You have within you that experience to say, "Water the seed and awaken me!"

Jesus, help us refuse to receive the testimony of death over our lives. We cannot receive it! We cannot receive it! We are not going to receive it! There is a greater power than the testimony of our natural eyesight. When we look out and we see things, our mind processes it in the natural, but we can look at the same thing with spiritual eyes and see something completely different.

That is exactly what happened at the pool. There was a natural testimony, a natural way of looking at things, and because of routine, so many accepted that. But there was another way of looking at the same situation: looking at it through the eyes of heaven. When the vision of heaven view a situation, it does not deny the reality, but it has a greater power, a superior law, that changes that situation and realigns it with the destiny of God. The enemy comes in and wants to distort and pervert the plan of God in our lives, but when we, as men and women of God, see that distortion taking place in people's lives, we must say, 'No!" We must say, "No! We cannot accept it, just because that's just the way it is. We cannot accept it because it's the way we've been told that it should be."

If vision is out of order, we must set it back in order. People are so hungry to walk in what they read about. When we read the scripture, people are so hungry for the reality of that. But so many times, when we read something and time goes by and it has not activated in our lives yet, then it begins to deceive us. That is why James spoke of being a doer and not just a hearer in James 1:25:

"But one who looks intently at the perfect law, the law of liberty, and abides by it, not having become a forgetful hearer but an effectual doer, this man will be blessed in what he does."

Here's the way that breaks down into deception: We see or read this word, but if we do not press in to it and see it activated, then man creates a doctrine around it that says, "Well, God does not do it anymore." They put the blame on God rather than take responsibility to press in for more. In our generation and lifestyle, if we see it and want it, we get it or we move on. But the Lord is saying, "Slow down! Look at it, and if it is not in line, put it in place. Press into it! Don't just jump onto the next chapter!"

If you always jump straight into the next chapter, you begin to build but you have skipped your foundation. When you do that, you build your house with improper plans, and then your house will be out of balance. There will be cracks and areas of weakness. That begins to describe some of our families and some churches. Please don't take that the wrong way. I am not speaking ill of the church. The church is who we are, the ecclesia. We are those who were called out by the voice of God. We also have to look at that situation, just like I said a minute ago. We examine it and we do not deny the situation, but we understand there is a superior law that applies to and supersedes it.

Chapter 1

INTRODUCTION TO THE APOSTOLIC MANTLE

In this teaching, we are going to introduce you to the apostolic mantle. We are going to present and expound on three key points. First, we are going to introduce the basic concept of the apostle. Next, we will define terms related to apostles and the apostolic work and function. Finally, we are going to explain exactly what apostles actually do. This is going to combat certain misunderstandings that have taken root in the Body of Christ, but we cannot be afraid to look at the Word, follow it, and teach what the Word actually says. I like to approach the Word of God very simplistically: what it says, I believe. Now I understand we have specific strategies for studying various topics. However, if that strategy causes us to eliminate vital tools or gifts God established in His Body, then His Body is weaker as a result. This limited thinking comes from a place of fear rooted mainly in a lack of understanding.

So let's dive into our topic. We all understand Jesus called and commissioned the twelve apostles. These were the initial apostles; they were the core leadership for the founding of the church. This early foundation was laid in Matt. 10:1-5, where Jesus called the disciples to Him and gave them authority:

"Jesus summoned His twelve disciples and gave them authority over unclean spirits, to cast them out, and to heal every kind of disease and every kind of sickness. Now the names of the twelve apostles are these: The first, Simon, who is called Peter, and Andrew his brother; and James the son of Zebedee, and John his brother; Philip and Bartholomew; Thomas and Matthew the

tax collector; James the son of Alphaeus, and Thaddaeus; Simon the Zealot, and Judas Iscariot, the one who betrayed Him. These twelve Jesus sent out after instructing them: 'Do not go in the way of the Gentiles, and do not enter any city of the Samaritans...'"

As we dig into this, you will notice that authority is a key component of the apostolic mantle. The level of authority that apostles carry within their God-assigned, sphere of influence is unmatched in many ways.

It is not possible to separate the ministry of an apostle from authority. If you have someone calling themselves an apostle without authority, then that person is not a true apostle. This does not mean that everyone who carries authority is an apostle. The first thing Jesus did when He called His twelve disciples/apostles was to grant them authority to drive out impure spirits, heal every disease and sickness, and declare the coming of the kingdom.

Notice that a sending forth and a commissioning of these apostles occurred here. Jesus sent them out and He told them where to go; He defined their sphere of authority. Every apostolic leader has a sphere of authority. Confusion comes in when we do not understand the sphere of authority that God has given. Not all apostles carry the same amount or sphere of authority. Every apostolic minister has a specific sphere of authority. If the apostle does not understand this principle and begins to cross over and try to take authority that has not been granted, it can often cause confusion. It is very important, as the people of God, that we understand this principle.

Jesus defined and set the boundaries for their sphere of apostolic authority. He told them not to deal with the Gentiles or enter any town of the Samaritans. That's a whole teaching by itself, but He restricted them to "the lost sheep of Israel." Every apostolic leader has a clearly defined sphere and also a clearly defined message. The message may shift depending upon the specific sphere of authority and commissioning. As you can see from the text above, Jesus restricted the disciples to proclaiming "...this message: the kingdom of heaven has come near." Their sphere of commissioning also included healing the sick, raising the dead, cleansing the lepers and driving out demons." These early apostles' message was supported by evidence: healing of the sick, raising the dead, cleansing the lepers, etc. There is always evidence confirming apostolic authority and ministry.

Chapter 2

WHAT IS AN APOSTLE?

The term apostle is translated *apostolos* in the Greek.[1] It is used seventy-nine times in the New Testament; Luke and Paul were responsible for sixty-eight of those occurrences. The term is specifically defined as "A messenger, an envoy, a delegate or one commissioned by another to represent the commissioner in some way, shape, form, or fashion- especially a person sent out by Jesus."[2] This term was not used in the realm of faith until Jesus used it to describe His followers. Originally, this secular term was used by the government. Jesus took a common term used by the Roman government and brought it into the realm of faith because it accurately defines the commissioning and function of an apostle.

Let me give you a brief explanation of what the term meant in the secular sense. When the Roman army conquered a specific area, those same troops occupied and held the territory. Later, when the leaders wanted to come in and inspect what had been conquered, they wanted to come into their own culture. They did not want to leave their Roman culture and go into a different area, so they created and sent a delegate called an apostle. This delegate, or apostle, would travel to the conquered territory and work to conform the region to the culture of Rome. The

---

[1] "Strong's Greek: 652. ἀπόστολος (apostolos) -- a Messenger, One Sent on a Mission, an Apostle," accessed April 07, 2018, http://biblehub.com/greek/652.htm.

[2] Bruce Cook, ed., Aligning With the Apostolic: An Anthology of Apostleship, vol. 1 (Lakebay, WA: Kingdom House, 2012).

communities defeated by the army had a completely different culture; the Roman government's apostles were culture transformers.

Jesus took the term and brought it into the church. When He called His twelve disciples apostles, He gave them authority to represent His kingdom to bring forth the message and culture of His kingdom in order to establish it. It's like Jesus gave them a blueprint of heaven and said, "This is the culture of heaven. You twelve men go into these towns and proclaim that the kingdom of heaven is at hand; it is within your grasp. Then demonstrate what happens when My kingdom comes and supersedes your culture." In other words, the apostles were to begin establishing the culture of heaven on the earth.

Think about the first two sentences of the Lord's Prayer in Matt. 6:9-10:

"Pray, then, in this way: 'Our Father who is in heaven, Hallowed be Your name. Your kingdom come. Your will be done, On earth as it is in heaven.'"

This prayer from Jesus is an apostolic commissioning. That message, or prayer, has become a tradition, and through this tradition, it has lost what it was intended to represent. However, God is raising up apostolic ministers to begin to declare a return to the foundations originally laid out in that prayer. This is the establishment of the culture of heaven, which is a greater, superior culture than what is here on earth. Heaven's culture looks like freedom from demons, freedom from sickness, freedom from oppression, and the opening up of blind eyes. You can read this through all four gospels, and the first five chapters of Acts before you find any mention of any other church office, officer, official, administrations, representations, or anything else church related. Even then, notice that the apostles took on that primary leadership role in addressing an issue in Acts 6:1-4:

"Now at this time while the disciples were increasing in number, a complaint arose on the part of the Hellenistic Jews against the native Hebrews, because their widows were being overlooked in the daily serving of food. So the twelve summoned the congregation of the disciples and said, 'It is not desirable for us to neglect the word of God in order to serve tables. Therefore, brethren, select from among you seven men of good reputation, full of the Spirit and of wisdom, whom we may put in charge of this task. But we will devote ourselves to prayer and to the ministry of the word.'"

Throughout the history of the church, there have been times of refreshing sent from heaven. Acts 3:19-21 speaks of the promise that God would send forth times of refreshing until the time or season of the restoration of all things:

"Therefore repent and return, so that your sins may be wiped away, in order that times of refreshing may come from the presence of the Lord; and that He may send Jesus, the Christ appointed for you, whom heaven must receive until the period of restoration of all things about which God spoke by the mouth of His holy prophets from ancient time."

That passage covers a long period of time in which restoration and seasons of refreshing would come forth from the Father. Each of these seasons blow on people and reinstitute the culture of heaven. Once each season gets established into the restoration move, there's another blowing of a wind of heaven that establishes another aspect of the culture of heaven or reenforces it.

19

There have always been seasons of restorations that come upon the Body of Christ. If we can study the move of God in a specific season, we can begin to understand how God wants us to walk in various areas. The move of God during a season is global, but there are smaller, national moves as well as smaller, regional moves within it. You should also note that while a wind of heaven or season of restoration may sweep through and ignite the flames of revival and awakening in one area, messengers often transport that same message into different regions. Jesus actually modeled this. Those around Jesus saw what He was doing: a season of refreshing had come upon Israel at that moment. Then, He sent those messengers, or apostles, out from His core region of ministry and said, "Now you take it into this town, and you take it into this town, and you take it into this town."

There has been a deep establishment of the apostolic ministry in different parts of the earth; those regions have experienced some of the greatest moves of God in the history of the world. India has almost surpassed any other area in the world in this way. There have been hundreds of thousands of churches planted and led by apostles. When Christianity began to bloom in China, the planting of house churches helped increase the percentage of the population who were Christian from almost nothing to surpassing 9.2% today.[3] That move was led by men and women who heard the call of God and identified themselves with the authority and call of an apostle.

---

[3] "China," Joshua Project, accessed April 07, 2018, https://joshuaproject.net/countries/CH.

Chapter 3

SIX KEYS TO TRANSITIONAL SHIFTS

When seasons of change begin to blow through an area, six specific stages can be mapped out.

Key #1 - Forerunning Voice of Call

The first stage involves a forerunning voice of the call. John the Baptist was that forerunning voice of call for the ministry of Christ and the advent of the New Covenant. He was sent to prepare the way for the emergence of the Messiah, the one promised in scripture. John the Baptist was of the old order (the Old Covenant), but he preached about a new season or time frame in Matt. 3:1-3:

"Now in those days John the Baptist came, preaching in the wilderness of Judea, saying, 'Repent, for the kingdom of heaven is at hand.' For this is the one referred to by Isaiah the prophet when he said, 'THE VOICE OF ONE CRYING IN THE WILDERNESS, MAKE READY THE WAY OF THE LORD, MAKE HIS PATHS STRAIGHT!'"

John 1:15 also confirms John as the forerunner for Jesus:

"John testified about Him and cried out, saying, 'This was He of whom I said, He who comes after me has a higher rank than I, for He existed before me.'"

The people had been waiting. Many of them kept waiting, because often when a long-term promise is being fulfilled upon a generation, people are more emotionally bound to the waiting more than to the fulfillment of the word.

What happened is that John came on the scene. He said, "Stop waiting! The Messiah is here!" Then he preached that same message. People came out to hear him, and one day he stuck out his hand and said, "Behold the Lamb of God!" He continued, "That's the one that I've been prophesying about! Now, it's time for Him to increase and me to decrease."[4] John 1:35-36 says:

"Again the next day, John was standing with two of his disciples, and he looked at Jesus as He walked, and said, 'Behold, the Lamb of God!'"

He was closing out the old order and releasing the New Covenant. There is a voice of call with a forerunner anointing. That voice of call and that anointing comes upon those who are able to discern what is just ahead for the Body of Christ. That is where the apostolic and prophetic ministries come together to work. The prophet sees it and doesn't know what to do with it. The apostle hears it and says, "Here's the blueprint. This is the structure. Now, let's run with it." There is a voice of calling, and this voice has been calling in America since the early 1900s.

Key #2 - Ability To Articulate The Shift

The second stage of divine, seasonal change is characterized by a new language that is released with the refreshing. For example, remember we just talked about the term: apostle. That

<hr>

[4] See John 3:30

term had never been used in the realm of faith until Jesus took it and said, "This is what we are going to use; this is how we are going to identify ourselves." A new language comes forth with every move of God.

Key #3 - A New Demonstration and Authority

A third important aspect of a seasonal change is different, divine manifestations. For example, the gifts of the Spirit begin to come forth, even though people may have been previously taught that they did not exist. As those spiritual gifts and divine manifestations emerge, believers' language changes in tandem with their understanding; their language has to line up with the truth. There is a demonstration and an understanding that grows when the forerunner call begins to declare that new season using the new language.

That what Jesus told the apostles to do things like heal the sick as they went forth. A demonstration comes forth that is very clear with every fresh move because God does not just release words without also releasing power; they are combined together. Therefore, when God releases a word, it shifts things in the natural realm which brings forth a demonstration because God births it in His people. Even He said He does not do a new thing unless He declares it to His prophets first in Amos 3:7.

"Surely the Lord God does nothing unless He reveals His secret counsel to His servants the prophets."

Someone has to prophesy it out; someone has to release that word. It comes from heaven by the Spirit of God. Then the new creation (those of us made new in the Spirit) prophesies it out. The elements have to line up with the word of heaven because it is a superior kingdom with a superior authority. A demonstration follows the forerunning voice and the newly refreshed language. When the demonstration comes about, those that just heard the word say, "Now I actually see it. It is happening!"

Key #4 - A New New Structure or Culture

This takes us to the next stage, which is when people begin to buy into what God is doing. This buy-in brings forth an acceleration of the new season's establishment. People are not having to process everything as quickly because the demonstration helps to provide evidence. Demonstration also helps to bring forth a new structure or housing, but I am not referring to a physical structure or building. I am describing a housing of understanding: a way of thinking.

Now that we have defined the term "apostle" and talked a little about the sequence of events that happens when God initiates a new season, I want to define the term "apostolic." The word "apostolic" refers to philosophies that typically originate with an apostle and helps to frame an understanding for the move of God. When God blows through a region with the winds of change, it begins to shake the way people think.

If you cannot give structure or house the understanding of a move, complete chaos results. Every revival in history started with massive chaos, but over time, it eventually came back into balance.

Key #5 - A New Balance

This stage of rebalancing is the next key on the list. As teachers begin to refine what has been learned in the new season, their work provides the framework that begins to house or encompass the move. They begin to understand the season from the word of God and say, "Now, here are the boundaries that the river needs to flow within." You can't have a river without banks; there are always banks. Parameters must come forth from heaven which carry the flow of God to guide the river.

Key #6 - A New Standard

Once the move has balanced and those parameters are understood, the season of refreshing has embedded itself in the overall move of restoration. This is when a new standard has replaced the previous standard which we operated by. This is the pace when the move or shift has been assimilated into our normal, daily lives. The shift is no longer an add-on to our Christian walk but is a fully, integrated part of who we are. Thus, the new standard has been formed and established.

Review The Six Keys of a Shift

When there is a divine shift in seasons, there is typically a forerunning voice of call. A new language emerges that develops from renewed understanding; demonstration aids the understanding. Then, a new structure or a new wineskin forms to house the understanding. The move sometimes goes from one extreme to another extreme before finding balance after the five-fold teachers and leaders have academic conversations and work together.

As a side note, we need to redeem the term "academic" from the dead dryness it is known for and actually use it properly. We can have different points of view, and we can discuss those different points of view because not one person has all of the understanding. These discussions from different perspectives and understandings are how the teachers begin to put this flow of a river inside proper, divinely-ordained boundaries.

Now, a new balance comes forth and ultimately, an advanced, new understanding of the standards in which Christians should walk is established.

Chapter 4

DEFINING TERMS IN AN APOSTOLIC COMPANY

The International Coalition of Apostolic Leaders (ICAL) was founded by Dr. C. Peter Wagoner several years ago when he began to understand that we were on the verge of an apostolic reformation. He had been watching shifts in the Body but was unable to discern exactly what God was doing. He said, "Okay, we don't all speak the same ways or say the same things. These apostolic leaders are looking different, but are very gifted." Then he began to bring together those with an apostolic call on their life, and they began to discuss the various shifts happening in the Body of Christ. As a result, they formed a coalition several years ago with Dr. Wagoner. Over the years, they have come to a better definition of the term "apostle." I want to present that updated definition to you now.

They define the term apostle as:

"A Christian leader gifted, taught, commissioned sent by God with an authority to establish the foundation government of the church within an assigned sphere."[5]

Our contemporaries have been walking in this a long time, and this is an agreed-upon definition. Now, the apostle's gifting and calling has many different expressions, and we are going to look at some of these expressions. Apostles are not clones of each other; we each have unique identities; we are diverse. We

---

[5] "About ICAL," International Coalition of Apostolic Leaders, accessed April 07, 2018, https://www.icaleaders.com/about-ical/.

have different spheres of authority, but most agree on the previous definition and the basic function of the apostle.

This definition is supported in several scriptures, such as in 1 Cor. 12:28:

"And God has appointed in the church, first apostles, second prophets, third teachers, then miracles, then gifts of healings, helps, administrations, various kinds of tongues."

This is the order that God set in the church but does not necessarily bring forth a hierarchical order. However, the first office is mentioned because it is vital in bringing about the others' healthy and effective functions. The Greek word used for "first" actually means "first in order." The word for "second" actually means "second" and "third" actually means "third." We do not need twelve different doctrines and debates to define one, two, and three.

Root of Fear During the Reformation

We have to ask ourselves why has this been overlooked for several hundreds of years. One reason it was overlooked was due of fear. This fear derived in part from the circumstances surrounding the Protestant Reformation. During those times, the pope was considered "The Apostle." So when those believers broke away from the Catholic church, they said, "No man is going to carry that kind of authority over us anymore!" They began to establish a doctrine that says, "The apostle doesn't exist anymore." That attitude and belief was founded in fear. We cannot operate from fear any longer but must move forward in faith. Problems will arise, but we carry enough authority to correct those problems.

Let's continue with the ICAL definition. It says,

"....by hearing what the Spirit is saying to the churches, by setting things in order accordingly for growth, maturity of the church...."[6]

This goes a little deeper than what we have seen so far. The definition first described what an apostle is, then how the calling happens, and continues by explaining the apostle's purpose. Apostles see the direction of or by the Holy Spirit, in partnership with prophets, and together, they lay the foundation for the building of the church.

Apostles of The Lamb

We know historically that there were twelve original apostles. That number was briefly reduced to eleven when Judas fell before being replaced by Matthias. These are considered the apostles of the Lamb. With that in mind, consider Rev. 21:14 where John describes the wall of the New Jerusalem (speaking of the city that comes down out of heaven):

"And the wall of the city had twelve foundation stones, and on them were the twelve names of the twelve apostles of the Lamb."

Therefore, the apostles of the Lamb were a unique group of twelve, not to be reproduced. This is where confusion exists. Do today's apostles carry that level of authority? I do not think we carry that level of authority; that was for twelve that were

---

6 "About ICAL," International Coalition of Apostolic Leaders, accessed April 07, 2018, https://www.icaleaders.com/about-ical/.

appointed at a specific time in history. So what about apostles today? Let's look at Ephesian 4:11-13:

"And He gave some as apostles, and some as prophets, and some as evangelists, and some as pastors and teachers, for the equipping of the saints for the work of service, to the building up of the body of Christ; until we all attain to the unity of the faith, and of the knowledge of the Son of God, to a mature man, to the measure of the stature which belongs to the fullness of Christ."

Jesus was the apostle, the prophet, the evangelist, the teacher, and the pastor. He carried all of those in one mantle. Essentially, He took that single mantle and divided it into five pieces at His ascension. That is how He brought interdependence within the Body of Christ. He said, "This one is going on the pastors, this one is going on the prophets, this one on the apostles, the teachers, and the evangelists."

Each five-fold minister walks in a specific sphere of authority granted by the Lord. Why? To equip His people for the works of service, so the Body of Christ may be built up. These five positions, or five callings, are to equip others in the Body of Christ, and then the Body of Christ is to do the work of the ministry. Five-fold ministers are equippers; they are not supposed to be the ones doing it all. They are called to train the large Body of Christ in how to walk in their identity, destiny, and calling. We can get real deep in that one word, "equip." It means "to set in order or to set in place." I do not have time to go much further than that here, but you can see that for yourself.

Therefore, the five-fold ministry is intended to equip the saints. The term "five-fold ministry" really is inaccurate because the ministry was given to the saints. We actually should say "five-fold equippers," but it will still work. So when will this team of five-fold equippers no longer be needed? The scripture we read above uses the word "until." Whatever condition or set of conditions follow that word is the standard we seek. If the "until" has not happened, then these gifts are still in operation. So five-fold leaders must work to equip believers until we all (as part of the Body of Christ) can rise to the conditions set forth in the scripture above. One of the most important goals is unity in the faith. It has not been reached, yet it is coming forth. It will happen; it is coming.

The passage also lists the "knowledge of the Son of God" and becoming "mature." That word "become mature" literally means "complete and lacking nothing." We understand there are still things that are lacking in the Body and in the kingdom, but we are not dwelling on those. Instead, we are prophesying the fulfillment: There will be no lack coming. We are moving towards the time when there will be no lack. Paul also mentions "obtaining the whole measure of the fullness of Christ."

Think about what the term "Christ' really means. It means "anointed one" or we can say "anointing." These ministers are going to be in place until the Body's built up and strong, we have reached unity of the faith and the knowledge of the Son of God is complete, and we are lacking nothing while walking in the full anointing. This is a deep revelation but one that I will not go deeper into with this specific teaching.

The definitions I have presented and am going to present come from an understanding, a general understanding, of the Word. I am not going to be able to point out twelve different verses that back up every definition, but remember, we are talking about a new language coming forth. It is a way that we can identify the concepts, in agreement, that we are talking about. We have to be able to say terms like "apostolic" and "apostolic culture" and fully understand what that means. We can't go into a teaching every time we communicate with someone and use a term like "apostolic culture." No, we want to come to an understanding of what these terms mean, and that is called building the structure of the house.

Apostolic Culture

Apostolic culture can be defined as the beliefs, attitudes, values, spiritual DNA, best practices, etc. that derive from association with an apostle.[7]

It is the grand sum of the influences brought about by an association with apostles or apostolic people. Remember, we talked about how Jesus took the term "apostle" from Rome. Used in the secular sense, Roman apostles were sent forth to establish the culture of Rome. Jesus appropriated the term and said, "We are going to use the term 'apostle' to refer to those who see the blueprint of heaven and work to establish it over the landscape and people of the earth." Establishing that blueprint brings about the culture of heaven.

It is a way of thinking. If you go into a church that does not embrace the prophetic or apostolic, then you will find a pastoral culture in place. It is so obvious that anybody can see it. A pastoral culture is not necessarily wrong; it is just incomplete. As God brings forth the apostles (as He has been aggressively since the late 1990s and early 2000s) and as those apostles arise and embrace their call, a shift is happening within the Body of Christ. In some places, you can walk in and sense the presence of heaven. More accurately, you can sense the presence of the one heaven was created around: God Almighty. That happens because the blueprint of heaven has been established with the help of the apostle.

---

[7] Bruce Cook, ed., *Aligning With the Apostolic: An Anthology of Apostleship*, vol. 1 (Lakebay, WA: Kingdom House, 2012), Glossary iv.

Therefore, apostolic culture is a way of thinking; it is a culture. It is not decorations, styles, or programs; it is culture, a way of thinking apostolically. An apostolic culture is one where the people have been released, taught, and brought about by one who carries the apostolic call. You can describe apostolic culture intellectually as it is something that you must have experienced. Only one that is called can teach experientially what that is. The same is true in regards to serving as a pastor. If you are not called as a pastor, you can understand the role yourself, but you cannot bring people into an experience of the anointing of a pastor because they do not have it. It takes a pastor to do that, just like it takes a prophet to release his/her anointing, and it takes a teacher to release a teaching anointing. So when I say, "this is an apostolic way of thinking," it is defining that culture.

Apostolic Gift

The term apostolic gifts refer to various supernatural gifts and enhanced natural abilities that empower apostles to function in their office effectively.[8] Apostles also release their gifting in the forms of impartation to others. The Holy Spirit brings these gifts and deposits them within a person, which helps that person function in their calling. You cannot function in any of these callings without the Holy Spirit empowering you. The apostles that Rome sent all carried authority but no supernatural power. The apostles sent by Jesus will carry a supernatural authority; it is a part of the gift-mix of the apostle.

Apostolic Function

---

[8] Cook, *Aligning With the Apostolic*, Glossary lxi.

33

Apostolic function is the application of apostolic principles that bring about the kingdom of God's design, order and activity to people, places and things.[9]

A call, apostolic or otherwise, is useless unless you function in it. A police officer carries a gun, but it is useless unless he uses it. That's what I am discussing. You can have an apostle, but if he does not function as one, no one receives the gift of his calling.

Apostolic Movement

Apostolic movement refers to a change of existing cultures, conditions, atmosphere, attitudes, beliefs, kingdom, government, norms, strategies, values, results, and outcomes brought about or precipitated by apostles or apostolic people.

Apostolic people house the understanding which they release. The movement happens when the understanding is released and conveyed from one place to another. That's what movement is. When you move from here, you are in a process, but where you stop, then you plant. An apostolic movement starts at a place and is brought about by teaching, impartation, and the gifts of an apostle. When people begin to grab that and run with it, a movement is formed.

Apostolic Company

An apostolic company is a people group who are influenced by the teaching of apostolic teams, apostles, etc. that catch it and begin to run with it.

---

[9] Cook, *Aligning With the Apostolic*, Glossary lxi.

We are in the seed of a movement in our region located in East Tennessee. In other regions, the movement is well manifested and carried out. In any case, this apostolic movement or company begins to shift ways of thinking, attitudes, and belief systems. It really shifts the powers of kingdoms. Where the enemy has set up a kingdom, a movement comes in and tears down the enemy strongholds establishing the strongholds of God or His way of thinking from heaven.

Apostolic Network

An apostolic network is a relational group, formally or informally affiliated, and led by apostles or apostolic, five-fold leaders.[10]

An apostolic network is a team of people that includes at least one apostle, although it can include several. They come together to form something and become members. They buy in with each other's calling and agree that they are going to run with this. The network will include disciples as well. You need to understand what I mean when I use the term "disciples" in this context. While we are all disciples of Jesus, not all are called into the five-fold function of leadership. In this context, disciples refer to individuals and leaders in the network who have chosen to align themselves in vertical or horizontal relationships with an apostolic leader and that leader's core values, vision, and common mission for a shared destiny and spiritual DNA.

Apostolic Spheres

---

[10] Cook, *Aligning With the Apostolic*, Glossary lxii.

So what do apostles do? We have to understand spheres of authority to answer that. Let's look at 2 Cor. 10:13-16:

"But we will not boast beyond our measure, but within the measure of the sphere which God apportioned to us as a measure, to reach even as far as you. For we are not overextending ourselves, as if we did not reach to you, for we were the first to come even as far as you in the gospel of Christ; not boasting beyond our measure, that is, in other men's labors, but with the hope that as your faith grows, we will be, within our sphere, enlarged even more by you, so as to preach the gospel even to the regions beyond you, and not to boast in what has been accomplished in the sphere of another..."

Paul was planting and watching growth. He planted under his sphere of authority, and as that sphere grew, so did his influence so he could go out further. I was talking to someone recently about how we walk in authority. However, when we go into churches that we have not planted, we do not get to boast of apostolic authority in those churches because they are not under our influence, unless they embrace us and the gifting we carry. It brings to mind Matt. 10:41:

"He who receives a prophet in the name of a prophet shall receive a prophet's reward; and he who receives a righteous man in the name of a righteous man shall receive a righteous man's reward."

For example, if a prophet comes into your house and you do not recognize him as a prophet. Instead, you recognize him as a teacher, you will get the reward of a teacher. If you recognize him as a prophet, you will get the reward of a prophet. The same is true with an apostle. In certain places we go, they do not recognize that authority. They see me as a pastor, and by their lack of understanding, they will not receive the gift an apostle carries. It's limited and puts a cap on what can be accomplished. That's what it means to recognize and receive the reward: if you embrace a person's call, then you receive the gift of what that person carries. This is the spirit of authority and how it functions.

Five-Fold Function

The concept of function is absolutely crucial. If a person is called as a five-fold leader in the Body of Christ, then they are called to function as such. For example, someone receives the calling to be a prophet. They are called, so they then begin to function. That initial function is an operation of the gift by grace. It's a gift because these are given by grace, not earned by merit.

The grace gift initiates the function of the calling in a person's life and allows them to begin to do that which they are gifted. However, they are not yet recognized by their peers; that comes later. This is so crucial to understand. While Andrea and I have been gifted for some time with an apostolic calling, when we first began functioning in that calling in Haiti, there was no public recognition of the apostolic calling. The fact that we were called as apostles meant nothing to anybody, but later, people began to recognize the office as we began to function in it. Now, we can go into a place and they will recognize it. That's what public and peer level recognition into a office is: the fruit and maturity of function.

You can have the call and the gift but be immature in it. When you are immature in it, you are not ready for public display. You are not yet recognized in the office, but the maturity comes as you function, as you learn, as you study, and as you listen to the Spirit of God. You are mentored by others in the office, then your maturity and your influence grows, and you begin to be recognized in the office. From that develops a greater level of authority. That is the purpose of ordination: people recognize God's hand on you in a certain area as you function. When that recognition happens, then there is a upper level or an apostolic level commissioning of a person into the office. Then, they get to walk in a greater recognized authority. The call itself is not really greater; it's the maturing of that original call.

This is exactly what happened with us in the last couple of years. We shifted streams, because if you are in a stream that does not recognize a calling or an office, you will never walk in the office. You can't do it because unbelief stops everything. Therefore, if a person believes that apostles and prophets are not active in the church today, then they cannot receive the reward of what the office carries. You just can't do it; unbelief cuts if off. When we shifted streams and began to be mentored and trained, the recognition began to come forth. With the recognition came a release of maturing and a greater function. The authority level increased.

Seven Mountains of Society

I want to give you a picture of how this idea of apostolic anointing can have a tremendous impact in society. If you that have been around our church or heard us speak, then you have probably heard someone mention the "Seven Mountains of Society." It's not a doctrine; it's just a way to view the various aspects of society. The word "mountains" here is describing cultural gateways or spheres of influence. These spheres of influence mold minds and shape behaviors. The seven mountains include family, education, business, government, media, arts/ entertainment, and religion.

The church is the starting point of kingdom function and transformation. For the church to fully impact society, it has to come outside of its four walls. The church houses the understanding and blueprint of heaven, but it releases that understanding into these six other areas. Out of our mountain of religion (or we can call it the mountain of faith), we send forth business owners who influence that area of society. We are going to dive further into that teaching later, but I firmly believe that God calls apostles, prophets, evangelists, pastors and teachers and thrusts them into business and other mountains of society.

If that does not happen, then the kingdom of God will never be fully manifested. Transformation can not take place on a global scale if we don't first function in these other mountains. When we just sit in the church, we are losing education. We are losing arts and entertainment along with these other areas. Here at Reach International Ministries,[11] we commission five-fold leaders into education; we commission them out as families. We send them forth into government, into media, into arts/ entertainment, etc. The church has neglected its responsibility to send forth these leaders into these other realms.

We like to sit back and talk about how much evil pours out of Hollywood. Is it so evil because we gave up our positional authority and said, "No, we just want to stay here in our protective little bubble?" God is saying, "No, there is coming a time...." and that is what the apostolic does. They look at these things and say, "Hey, we are sending you over there. Take that mountain in Jesus' name!" And boom, you are sent and covered. You are commissioned with authority to go and establish the kingdom of God. If we do not do this, we can't just sit back and pray. We have a responsibility to also go into those areas.

R.A.I.N. - Reach International

---

[11] For more info, go to *RainNetwork.org* or *RNetwork.org*.

We are in the early stages of our apostolic network here in the states, but we have had international partnerships for several years. We are seeing great hunger from the body of Christ for relational networks with like-minded people rallied around vision. As a result of a major shift in the body of Christ, many people are coming into alignment with our apostolic network and others. Our network is called R.A.I.N: Reach Apostolic International Network. The name comes from a prophecy I gave in Haiti in 2017. I began prophesying that God was raising up rain centers across the country of Haiti; a rain center is where a spiritual outpouring and resulting awakening is happening. Deut. 32:2 uses that terminology as well:

"Let my teaching drop as the rain, My speech distill as the dew, As the droplets on the fresh grass And as the showers on the herb."

There will be questions on function that we all have, but what we have to do is learn to ask those questions and have open discussions within relationships. It is important to have open conversations on things like this so we don't erode trust or the underlying belief system. While the apostolic paradigm is new to many, we do not have to go and defend everything, but we do welcome academic discussions. Notice, I did not say debate but discussion of different points of view.

Value in Diversity

If you get one hundred apostles together in a room, you are going to have one hundred, diverse applications of a common call because God is diverse and filters His calling through your unique personality. Even with diversity, you still have a common-core, apostolic function and way of thought. Similarly, if you put one hundred pastors in a room, you would find that their core function is the same while their application and strategies are each unique because of their diverse personalities, education and experiences.

This is why we are able to have open discussions and conversations at proper times. As God grants us greater influence for an apostolic company to arise in its fullness and calling, there must be strong equipping which is why we are making such an emphasis in this area. We will continue to bring out teachings on family structure, family dynamics, and good communication. Those things will happen, but most of us come from a background where all we have heard is messages centered around good family, good character, and church attendance. These issues are important, and I am not diminishing their importance, but when God emphasizes something in the Body, we must emphasize it. That's how we walk with Him. The office of the pastor has dominated for the last hundred two hundred years. We understand it; we get it. What we don't get is how it functions well with the apostle and the prophet, but the reason is due to a lack of communication between those functions.

As we communicate, trials will come as well as errors because we begin to walk in an area that has not been well established in our region. Therefore, we are going to learn how to walk these things out in a team environment which goes down to the foundation of trust and relationships with each other. When we trust each other, then we can ask, "How do you understand this topic or application?" and understand we are not going to be pounced on, ridiculed, or embarrassed. This atmosphere even allows someone to have a dissenting voice about something, but trust and relationships are key. They allow us to understand those questions and realize that dissenting voices are not coming from a place of condemnation or rebellion. In other words, if there are things that need to be expressed. If you see an area and say, "I don't get this." Then, I can teach on it. I may not fully understand it, but I am okay with not understanding. I can study. I can talk to mentors. I don't know all this, but I am also not afraid to begin walking in something that God is doing. Let's walk this path together.

Chapter 5

Apostolic Expressions

Activate and Impart

Apostles activate and impart. Paul mentions this aspect of his ministry when writing to the Romans in Rom. 1:11:

"....For I long to see you so that I may impart some spiritual gift to you, that you may be established."

Paul said he was wanting to visit the Romans to impart some spiritual gifts to them. Later, in 1 Tim. 4:14, Paul speaks of a spiritual gift given by prophecy and through the laying on of hands. Paul understood a part of his apostolic calling was to impart and activate others into their spiritual gifting and calling.

Impartation takes place in several ways, but I will give you an example in my own personal life. Early in my calling, I had desired the prophetic gifting to flow in my life, so I began to seek out those that were operating in that gifting. I went to a ministry about an hour drive from where I was living, and right after I entered the service, the pastor/leader called me out to come to the front. He began to prophesy over me, and this was the first time I had been prophesied as a trailblazer and a pioneer. When he finished, he laid hands on me and released in my life an activation of the prophetic. I left there, and as I was driving home and thinking, things started stirring in my spirit.

I began to pray as I drove home that evening. As I prayed, I could see people in my spirit, and I had prophetic words coming into my mind for them. Before I arrived home about an hour later, I had called someone and said, "Can I prophesy over you?" Right then, I began prophesying over her, and since that time, I have prophesied over thousands of people. This was a result of impartation and activation that began that night though. It was not just a laying on of hands and a declaration, but an activation also came forth. This is one example of the power of impartation.

Many of you carry gifts that have yet to be activated and released, but in the right type of setting, where equipping and teaching are happening, understanding can come forth. When that happens, it is like you have dug out the well, and then a free flow emerges of the deposit God has already placed within you. However, there is another principle that bears mention to.

Paul, as Timothy's spiritual father, wrote separate letters encouraging and exhorting him. In the first, he spoke of the gift that had been imparted to him by the elders in 1 Tim. 4:14:

"Do not neglect the spiritual gift within you, which was bestowed on you through prophetic utterance with the laying on of hands by the presbytery."

After an impartation happens, an activation must follow. Sometimes we buy into a lie that if we just come to church and hear the word preached, we will grow. That lie creates within us a deception preventing us from activating and using what we have been taught. It is vitally important that we use the gifts that God has given us. The season of one person doing everything is quickly coming to an end.

Apostles Pioneer

The third thing that apostles do is receive revelation and pioneer. One example of this is recorded in Acts 16:9-10:

"A vision appeared to Paul in the night: a man of Macedonia was standing and appealing to him, and saying, 'Come over to Macedonia and help us. When he had seen the vision, immediately we sought to go into Macedonia, concluding that God had called us to preach the gospel to them."

Notice that the revelation came by vision, followed by the decision to pioneer a work in a new region. This is the Lord orchestrating Paul's steps and leading him. We may have an encounter similar to this and dismiss it if we have not been equipped to hear and listen to what the Lord saying. Notice though, after Paul had seen the vision, he got ready immediately to leave for Macedonia, concluding or interpreting that God had called him to preach the gospel in that region.

It is important to notice the difference here between how the prophetic and the apostolic mantles function, and both of them are right. If a prophet receives a vision or word like this, they are going to get up, gather together other prophets or intercessors, and begin to pray about it. When an apostle receives something like this, they get up and immediately bring forth action. That is why the two gifts balance out each other so well. An apostle is going to be building and moving; they are going to be doing something. On the other hand, a prophet is going to be in intercession much of the time.

That is the gift they carry: prophetic intercession. So if the two are not working together, the apostle is going to advance too quickly without prayer, and the prophetic is more likely to spend too long in prayer concerning the next step without moving. However, when the two serve and operate together, strong foundations are built. This is one of the reasons the Lord has given five-fold ministry gifts. If there were only one or two, we would be out of balance. But when we are receiving from each of them, a greater and more well-rounded balance happens within the Christian life.

Apostles Build and Birth

Paul wrote about the importance of this in 1 Cor. 3:10:

"According to the grace of God which was given to me, like a wise master builder I laid a foundation, and another is building on it. But each man must be careful how he builds on it."

This was Paul describing his gift to the Corinthians. He is saying that he laid the foundation, but others actually built on it. If Paul had not understood his gift, he may have got jealous when others began to build on it. But he understood his purpose in that region: to prepare the way for others to build upon the foundation.

We understand that each gift complements other gifts, but we cannot just operate in one. For example, we have always had a loose network of people affiliated with us, especially in Haiti. However, the Lord began dealing with me quite a while back about establishing a more organized network. Organization is not a bad term. It's a very good term when it is put within its proper context. For example, Ezekiel spoke about the bones coming together, bone upon bone, and then flesh and muscle grew over those bones in Ezek. 37:7-8:

"So I prophesied as I was commanded; and as I prophesied, there was a noise, and behold, a rattling; and the bones came together, bone to its bone. And I looked, and behold, sinews were on them, and flesh grew and skin covered them; but there was no breath in them."

If there is lack of structure, then weakness occurs within the structure because the bones are the structure to which the muscles attach themselves and operate. Therefore, this is why the Lord began dealing with me about really setting into place our network in Haiti.

Let's continue with this concept of building and birthing from revelation. We read in Eph. 2:19:

"So then you are no longer strangers and aliens, but you are fellow citizens with the saints, and are of God's household,"

You and I house the very presence of God. We are the temple that is being built together out of living stones, but we are not built independently. God designed a body of believers; we are interdependent upon each other for our growth, safety, and health. While one belongs to this part of the Body over here and knows how to function, another one somewhere else knows how to function differently. I know we have heard this teaching, but it must come forth in practical application in a way that builds up the body. When we connect in apostolic and prophetic ministry and receive those gifts, we see an activation of Matt.10:41:

"He who receives a prophet in the name of a prophet shall receive a prophet's reward; and he who receives a righteous man in the name of a righteous man shall receive a righteous man's reward."

We can all quote that scripture, but what is the reward of a prophet? If he is an equipper (as Ephesians 4 says he should be), he equips the Body in the ability to both see and hear. That is the gift that he brings. If you receive an apostle in the name of an apostle, you receive an apostle's reward. It's a principle. The gift

47

received from the apostle is the ability to be set into place and to function causing an easier path. It is not stressful and does not wear you out because when you are doing what you were designed to do. However, if my shoulder tries to operate like my knee, it will not function properly and will be out of order. Apostles set things in order which bring forth the next stage of building within the house of God.

Here is another thought to consider. When John the Baptist came onto the scene, the Pharisees went out and asked him if he was actually Elijah, who they believed would physically return to Earth in John 1:19-23:

"This is the testimony of John, when the Jews sent to him priests and Levites from Jerusalem to ask him, 'Who are you?' And he confessed and did not deny, but confessed, 'I am not the Christ.' They asked him, 'What then? Are you Elijah?' And he said, 'I am not.' 'Are you the Prophet?' And he answered, 'No.' Then they said to him, 'Who are you, so that we may give an answer to those who sent us? What do you say about yourself?' He said, 'I am A VOICE OF ONE CRYING IN THE WILDERNESS, MAKE STRAIGHT THE WAY OF THE LORD,' as Isaiah the prophet said."

Later, Jesus said of John that he was the Elijah who was to come in Luke 7:24-27:

"When the messengers of John had left, He began to speak to the crowds about John, 'What did you go out into the wilderness to see? A reed shaken by the wind? But what did you go out to see? A man dressed in soft clothing? Those who are splendidly clothed and live in luxury are found in royal palaces! But what did you go out to see? A prophet? Yes, I say to you, and one who is more than a prophet. This is the one about whom it is

written, "BEHOLD, I SEND MY MESSENGER AHEAD OF YOU, WHO WILL PREPARE YOUR WAY BEFORE YOU.'"

Consider this: John the Baptist, a prophet called by God, only understood a limited portion of his calling. He said, "I am the voice of the one crying in the wilderness, but I am not the Elijah who is to come." Jesus later corrected that and said John was the Elijah who was to come.

As members in the Body of Christ, we may understand one function or aspect of our call. We may understand a portion of our call, but when the other five-fold ministries can speak into our lives, they may call us forth into the next level of that calling. John said, "I am the voice of one crying in the wilderness but I am not the one who is to come." Jesus stepped in and said, "You are the Elijah who is to come." John had a limited understanding of his function within the Body, but Jesus had a greater understanding. That's exactly what happens when we come into alignment with the apostolic ministry: things get set in order which releases a greater function and calling of the Body of Christ.

Apostles Send

"Then it seemed good to the apostles and the elders, with the whole church, to choose men from among them to send to Antioch with Paul and Barnabas—Judas called Barsabbas, and Silas, leading men among the brethren." Acts 15:22

Apostles are senders. They are sent ones themselves and understand how to thrust forth others in the same manner. A divine acceleration occurs with apostolic ministry, because apostles see a place in need of a specific gift within the body of Christ. When they see the gift activated, they direct it to the place where it is needed. They send forth and declare, "You are needed there." This awards the person with fulfillment and freedom because he or she may not be functioning so well where they currently are. However, when they step into the place where their gifting is needed with faith, they receive the reward of an apostle and begin to function well. They begin to function where they were designed to function which benefits the whole body.

For years, we have had pastors, who were great men of God, leading local churches as they should but were not connected with prophetic and apostolic elders. Thus, we have raised up a generation of believers that are very well protected and cared for, but as a result, they are also weak and anemic in power. No divine thrust has occurred: no divine commissioning and no setting in order. That is because a pastor's gift is to protect, shepherd the sheep, and care for them. A pastor typically wants to protect so much that he will not want to release the sheep. If the sheep are with him, then he can use his gifting to protect them well, but he sometimes holds onto them longer than he should.

When that happens, the sheep may start operating or functioning outside of their gifting and thus get out of order, resulting in chaos. However, the apostolic person, if they are welcome into that house, can look at that pastor and say, "You've done well raising them up, but now it is time to thrust them out and advance the kingdom. They are fat and well cared for. They are healthy. Now, let them get out, start running, and become lean." That decision then brings order, and they begin to function well.

It is important to note that none of these offices function well without trust. Trust brings acceleration. If there is no trust, then bickering and war break out. One breaks off from another and the Body is stunted once again, but that does not happen as much when apostles can send people forth. They align people and generations and see things through the sphere of their calling. They see things from the distance and are able to pull back because they see the larger picture.

Let me use this illustration: pretend that each of you is blindfolded and led into a room where an elephant is standing. You fumble your way up to its tail and are asked, "What is an elephant like?" Based on that experience (the feeling of the tail), you describe it like a large rope. Another person finds the creature's front leg and describes it like a big tree trunk." Another touches its side and says it feels like a big wall. Each person is correct in their description of the elephant, but all of them are still limited in their understanding and perspective.

This is exactly what happens with many ministers in the Body of Christ if they are localized and disconnected. In their limited scope of vision, they are being good shepherds but are not connected to those who have the ability to draw back and see the larger picture. Thus, they miss out on the larger perspective of the Body of Christ. The apostolic gift affirms that each one is right in his own perspective, but that perspective may be limited. The apostle connects each person to his/her proper place by each gifting and calling thus causing the bigger picture of what God is doing to form at the regional, national, and even global level.

None of our ministries are truly independent but are interdependent upon each other. What do apostles actually do then? They align people and generations. Before I ever began to understand this principle, I would separate people in our national conferences by their generations and ask them to bless each other. We would try to get them to understand that they all look different and do things differently, but it is still the same Holy Spirit working within. Each person is the answer to the other's prayers if only one can understand it. This generation is praying for wisdom and for an awakening, but the awakening they are praying for is dormant inside the next generation. It can only be awakened with the wisdom that they are carrying, and they must be interdependent on each other.

The apostolic has the ability to step back and look at the entire situation and instruct: "This needs to be poured in here, and this should be poured in there, etc." Honor will bring forth the release of wisdom, and wisdom will bring forth the awakening of the promise. However, it all works together, but without perspective, we become very localized and very protective. They must work together. Look at the way Paul spoke to the church in Corinth in 1 Cor. 4:14-15:

"I do not write these things to shame you, but to admonish you as my beloved children. For if you were to have countless tutors in Christ, yet you would not have many fathers, for in Christ Jesus I became your father through the gospel. Therefore I exhort you, be imitators of me. For this reason I have sent to you Timothy, who is my beloved and faithful child in the Lord, and he will remind you of my ways which are in Christ, just as I teach everywhere in every church."

Paul was a father to Timothy. We know that, but Paul did not keep Timothy close. He thrust him forth, but Paul still extended his influence over Timothy. He was a covering to him. If Timothy had just walked in to the Church at Corinth without Paul's endorsement, he may have walked in with only a gift, but gift would not have had the chance to activate without Paul's influence. When Paul said, "I have sent you Timothy. Receive him; he is my son," he granted Timothy his own influence.

Think about that: if we have a person come to us saying he has a message, we may not discern that very quickly. But if my spiritual father says, "Mike, I have a son in the area and I would like for him to come and release something among you," then my spiritual father is extending his covering over that person.

Thus, we would let him walk in and allow him to speak because a father extends his influence over those around him. He grants them a covering and also an enabling.

If you think of this in terms of function versus office, Timothy would have had the ability to function, but he would have not been able to because he was not recognized in the office. When Paul sent this letter and told the Corinthians, "I have sent Timothy to you; receive him," he granted Timothy the opportunity to function within his office. This is a picture of what fathers do: they extend their covering. Not long ago, I released a blessing over one of my spiritual sons at a conference. I was sending him out to some churches, and I wanted those pastors to receive him. We blessed him and extended influence over him. I said to the pastors, "He is my son and has this gift. When he comes to your church, receive him."

Now, they are excited for him to come although they understand his limited level of maturity. They are going to receive him at that level and are going to have an expectation of his ability to function, but they are not receiving him as the full office of an apostolic leader as they would receive me.

Apostles Release The Supernatural

Apostles will carry forth supernatural manifestations, signs, and wonders. A wonder is just that: it makes you wonder. They will also plant churches, appoint and oversee local church pastors or elders, settle disputes in the church, and apply discipline. This discipline can include excommunication, which is really lacking. They also attract and distribute financial resources, cast out demons, and break curses.

Just because a person may function in one or more of these areas does not mean they are an apostle. Additionally, you may have an apostle that does not function in all of these areas because each minister carries a unique gifting and sphere of authority. James, an apostle in Jerusalem, spoke clearly and decisively when settling a doctrinal dispute. However, there is no indication that he carried authority over all of these people. However, he did carry an authority to convene apostolic elders indicated in Acts 15:6, 13:

"The apostles and the elders came together to look into this matter....After they had stopped speaking, James answered, saying, "'Brethren, listen to me....'"

When he called people to come in, they came in, but there is no indication of him having some kind of a hierarchical authority over them. He carried an ability to convene them together.

Some apostolic leaders will indeed carry a hierarchical authority for people that choose to come under them and relate to them, not by a legal authority but by a relational authority. Apostolic authority is based on the ability to build relationships. A person may choose to come under one's covering because of that relationship, and many apostolic leaders will only have the ability to have that close relationship with thirty, forty, or fifty people. However, if an apostolic team is active, that team can cover hundreds to maintain a growing relationship.

Closing Thoughts

I want you to take courage: God is doing big things within our world today. We are living in one of the greatest times to be alive. Yes, many things seems to be changing very quickly in our world, but God is positioning His people to bring forth a major shift within Christianity. The Kingdom of God is advancing at an unprecedented pace, and you and I are a part of it.

With many five-fold ministers connecting throughout the body of Christ today, it is imperative that you also get connected. I encourage you to find a church or ministry that embraces and values the teaching of all five-fold ministers. By connecting with a true apostolically-aligned ministry or church, you will be positioned to grow into all God has called you to be.

Please connect with us on our website at RNetwork.org or RainNetwork.org and check out our other equipping resources. If you are interested in having us speak on this topic or other topics at your church, conference or event, please contact us directly at Mike@RNetwork.org.

Many Blessings,
Mike and Andrea Brewer

End Notes

1. "About ICAL." International Coalition of Apostolic Leaders. Accessed April 07, 2018. https://www.icaleaders.com/about-ical/.

2. Cook, Bruce, ed. *Aligning With the Apostolic: An Anthology of Apostleship*. Vol. 1. Lakebay, WA: Kingdom House, 2012.

3. "China." Joshua Project. Accessed April 07, 2018. https://joshuaproject.net/countries/CH.

4. *New American Standard Bible.* La Habra, CA: Lockman Foundation, 1995.

5. "Strong's Greek: 652. ἀπόστολος (apostolos) -- a Messenger, One Sent on a Mission, an Apostle." Accessed April 07, 2018. http://biblehub.com/greek/652.htm.

Made in the USA
Columbia, SC
27 February 2025

54498710R00033